Phantom Limb

David Musgrave was born in Sydney in 1965, and lives there. He is the author of the novel *Glissando: a Melodrama*, the critical study *Grotesque Anatomies: Menippean Satire Since the Renaissance* and three previous collections of poetry. He is the publisher at Puncher and Wattmann and lectures at the University of Newcastle.

Phantom Limb

DAVID MUSGRAVE

JOHN LEONARD PRESS

First published 2010 by
John Leonard Press
PO Box 443, St Kilda, VIC 3182

© David Musgrave, 2010

This book is copyright. Aside from fair dealing for the purposes of study, research, criticism, review, or as otherwise permitted under the Copyright Act, no part may be reproduced by any process without written permission. Inquiries should be addressed to the publisher.

National Library of Australia
Cataloguing-in-Publication data:

Musgrave, David, 1965 –.
Phantom Limb
ISBN 978 098 052 69 9 8
1. Title.
A821.4

Design: Sophie Gaur
Photo: James Ostinga
Printed and bound by BPA Print Group, Burwood, Victoria

Set in Goudy

ACKNOWLEDGEMENTS

Poems in this collection have appeared in the following publications:

Bathyspheric Review, The Best Australian Poetry 2006 (ed. Judith Beveridge, UQP), *The Best Australian Poems 2009* (ed. Robert Adamson, Black Inc) *Blast, Blue Dog, Crannog, The Honey Fills the Cone: Newcastle Poetry Prize Anthology 2006, Journal of Australian Studies, Literature & Aesthetics, Mad Hatter's Review, Meanjin, The New Yorker, Perihelion, Snorkel, Southerly, The Puncher & Wattmann Anthology of Australian Poetry* (ed. John Leonard, 2009), *The Sydney Morning Herald, Thylazine,* and *Time's Collison with the Tongue: 2000 Newcastle Poetry Prize Anthology.*

Some of these poems appeared in *To Thalia* (Five Islands Press) and *Watermark* (Picaro Press).

'The Baby Boomers' won the 2008 Newcastle Poetry prize. 'Lagoon' won the Broadway (Poets Union) Poetry Prize in 2001. An earlier version of this book won the Alec Bolton Prize for best unpublished manuscript in 2008.

CONTENTS

To Jill Dimond

&

Peter Kirkpatrick

God be gracious to Musgrave, for he is a Merchant

Christopher Smart, *Jubilate Agno, fragment* C

Open Water

At last we got clear of the narrows
and headed out into open water,
shredding the rapid ocean into spray
until time became something that tasted
of salt, open like a sentence:
beat up, beat down, iambic swell.

Then the horizon downed the final wafer
of land and we entered the massive rocking
stillness of the deep and its sparking
serrations, shut down the engines and drifted.
The sun beat on everything, bleaching
the top of the sky and its anvils

of cloud and lit up the leap of flying fish,
like daytime meteors, darning the sea.
We were still and unalone. Trawlers
far to north chugged stern-heavy
back to port, and beyond them tankers,
languorous sunbathers stretched out and waiting.

Out of this same illimited plain
the British had come, wind-stung and flawed
and laden with cargoes of concepts
and shadows, things which couldn't be seen
but assembled themselves, a ruling machine
intricated into the vast and difficult continent-factory,

and worked out in angles of apple-bright
metals, a lunar rust and starbursts
of roads and houses and human geometries,
varicose gullies and othering fences,
the bullet's graph. These were the blood-lessons:
that something which does not yet exist

is not the same as nothing: folded deep
within ourselves are nuggets of future
and the shock of their dredging.
Sunlines speared the water as we tilted
and sprawled and trailed a line
and let currents age us, gently.

There were only two ways to go:
across to where we had been, would go,
or down, each almost forever.
But even the longest line will turn,
like our slow drift
leaving its scrawl on open water.

Aubade

Morning shadows are the best,
they stretch my masks along the hall
and frame book cover portraits with tiling
light and scalene
before they tilt up and back
into the street. All is forgiveness and clean,
the traffic like a nervous rehearsal
cough and, down on the street, schoolgirls discover
red bull and coffees
and the birds, exhausted by triggering dawn
now strut the pavement, wings tucked back like floorwalkers,
little pleased nibs sketching the air.

A Glass of Water

Un seul verre d'eau éclaire le monde Cocteau

Behind the wedding couple, a mirror harbours
their reception.
Outside, from the verandah, the harbour mirrors
the exception
of city from sky, hills snug with houses

and a glass of water standing on the railing,
half empty or half full. In the failing

afternoon light
brightening buildings counterpoint the darkness,
glinting upside-
down inside the glass, and the newly-weds,
seen from outside

joining hand to hand for the wedding reel,
glide under its meniscus, head over heels.

Grieving

there was a long tumultuous shouting sound like the voice of a thousand waters Poe

1.

. . . beginning as a stillness
by a window, perhaps with the sting
of a tear, or a gentle rocking
which becomes by degrees more agitated
until the desire to break the window
and leap out or fall back
from the transom and retreat further inside
where a savage wrecking takes place,
so complete, in fact, that it involves you
running from a burning, collapsing edifice,
yourself stumbling and falling
but obsessed by the impossibility
of grieving —

2.

is like cramming words back into your mouth
after having said, like Cassandra,
what cannot be unspoken, except it's a thing
that cannot be unthinged;
or like tracing a river back to its source,
the mountain stream, where trees snag wind
and the clouds hedge the peak
and into nowhere a trickle devolves and disappears.
It's another place where words begin.

Phantom Limb

My enemy reminds me of my father:
the smell of smoke and newsprint, and the eye

behind the lens. I cannot understand the likeness:
my father was kind,

but he, my enemy,
deceives me from his empty office;

besides, my father has been dead for fourteen years.
I haven't seen my enemy for one,

but a semblance persist. He is a length of mind
which has no end. He harvests anger

and his name is myth.
His limbs hang loose and powerless,

his reasons, features, falter into word-mist,
but still he hurts me with his snarling smile.

I dreamt of him the other night
— wood is ash's dream of being whole —

and when I woke, the only clue
to what I'd lost, like a tingling nose before the lie

was an itch where nothing itched before,
a phantom absence: the limb I never knew I had, excised.

Puddles

Before we met I used to walk for miles
each time it rained,
plashing myself through the teeming city
and its angry offscourings,
the wet footprints of the sky.

In those long, cold mirrors, diamond-shallow,
I saw my flattened stride
into the future of another puddle,
mussel soup, with which I courted

you one night, having forgotten how one puddle
leads always to another,
inchmeal deep

like windows stretched across the ground
and behind them, in their stillness,
the sudden pooling of our lives.

Grass

As I waded through paddocks of wallaby grass, nineawn,
windmill, umbrella, and curly Mitchell, I remembered
how I had felt like ripping my own face off.

I'd just flown through a free-fall
of stomach-unseating violence
from the city to a western plain and survived

for my annual face-off with *bucolia melancholia.*
I wandered there in a kind of grateful silence.
A powdery mind-black ribbon of falling

dark water was looping around from the south,
nudging trees like a dog's black nose
with wet, cold wind

and then as it closed in, the sky's white mouth
opened, hushed then bawled once in a decade rain.
Channels flexed their muddy sinews

and out in the dust-red yard
the earth spat up echoes of rain
and the slow leaks sped in the homestead roof's groined hollows.

When the rain cleared
the dense cloud had passed into a fine dust haze
discing the sun. New cloud roped

and five-minutes-to-seed grass
began to shoot
as the house was lowered slowly into darkness.

The oil-black smoke from the ululating flames
of the citronella lamps curled and awned
as I flickered inside the house

where the talk was of grass
and of making a killing
and where we would feast.

Soil

The earth is growing in me, clump by clump,
a butting fastness, anchoring but intimate
as a scar, an out of bounds moving in.
Perhaps that's why dreams take longer,

lately, to wander out of, as morning tilts at noon
and hope resumes its blind battering.
Soon orbs of wet clay, once eyes
will scan and frame in this cave of bone

but until then I'll keep on losing balance
as if half of me were air, the other ink
for a small obituary, or a small grimoire,
a B-grade movie prop scripted to burst into flame.

Storm

Her absence was needless but necessary, like rain
when the blue sky cools
before a wetting wind and the horizon
closes like a fist against your mouth
as if helping you grieve for a ripe trauma:
that pineapple exploding across the sky,
only it's a cloud spilling over the corner
of a large building and rain wheeling
around from vertical to seven
o'clock and beyond, in your face
as it gusts low and up from the heaven
of the gutter and nooses you
with ice-cold droplets, followed by spider-fingers
of water down your back and the reek
of the street fumes straight up
and as the return of a sweaty blue
shoal-ridden sky allows you to cross
the road moderately shattered by traffic
only the present matters,
the sure clearing sky,
the way steam always rises,
stains always stiffen, shrink, vanish.

On the Inevitable Decline into Mediocrity of the Popular Musician who Attains a Comfortable Middle Age

O Sting, where is thy death?

Sirens, Waverley Cemetery

Container ships
coming in from the east,
cargo shifting
in sullen swell,

hear nothing
from those dirty-white lips
pledged,
with soot-edged

wings of stone,
on the windswept hill
in attitudes the colour of bone.
They sing no song that cannot be

ignored, not even in the surety
of silence, there on the hill at Waverley.

Clouds, Lake Titicaca

Toad clouds hover over low water;
staggering thunderheads scrape their bellies
on glowering mountains, old fat dogs
twitching rain.

By th'mass and 'tis, like a camel indeed.

Duck clouds in living room
wall formation line up for the puff! puff!
of poachers over the horizon. Flat-bottomed
cumuli putter across the lake.

Methinks it is like a weasel.

The surface of the lake loves clouds the way hinges
love a door, like the way sky folds
into trees at night. Clouds at night are shaggy
heads of Titans, eyebrows, furious manes

It is backed like a weasel.

by dawn plastered to pink striations
of ice-cream cake. Climbing the sky
the sun is a confident politician
and clouds flee. This is no time for shadows.

Or like a whale

But every afternoon they forget, moussing themselves
in the lake's mirror, then slouching
towards Oblivia, Bolivia, humpbacked
and diving rebelliously upward
into deep blue

Very like a whale

Young Montaigne Goes Riding

Que scais-je?

I wake up to the sound of music played
on pipes or strings — my father's whim, not mine.
He believes my tender brain might bruise
if I wake too suddenly. Saturnine
cows orbit his estate and confuse
themselves with a grove's piebald shade.

It's early. Bullish nostrils quivering steam.
Dew-shuddering trees and a clatter of stallions.
Stuttering chickens peck and servants scrub
flagstones, an armada of grey galleons
scouring shallows. One of them, a snub-
nosed woman, I recall — that is, I seem

to recall, for I have no memory to speak
of, only curiosity — comes from the same
village on my father's estate where I
was put out to nurse. I greet her by name.
Mornings like these, before the sun gets high,
I like to ride: and I prefer the oblique

paths which wander and meander to the one
which goes straight to the truth. Mist rises
from the fields, all patchwork, like our deeds,
and we ride. How one exercises
one's judgement choosing a suitable steed
is a question worthy of a theologian:

do we judge a horse when racing or at rest
in the stable? And how do we judge a king:
upon the throne of state, or on that private
throne, his private estate? I read the steaming
dollops falling from the jouncing nates
of my companion's horse as I would a text

of somc thousands of words, theorising
on the consistency of excrement
and what it tells us of the teeth, the heart,
the firmness of the gut and the contentment
and the clearness of a conscience. The fart
is a different matter: a vapid, rank uprising

disproving the obedience of the anus
as it is discussed in Vives' commentary
on Augustine's man who synchronised
his farting to the steady alimentary
metre of verses that his friends devised.
Usually it is most unruly and mutinous —

much like our current form of government.
I am fortunate to be born in depraved times:
for very little effort I am thought
virtuous; abstaining from the crimes
which are the weapons of that war fought
here, in the hub of civil discontent,

allows me idle hours, time which breeds
chimeras and grotesque things. Variety
alone satisfies me. We pass a field
of sheaves of wheat whispering like a society
of academicians. Weighed down by their yield
they learn humility and lower their heads,

but in the next field ears of wheat rise high
and lofty, heads erect and proud as they
are empty. What do I know? That I can't bear
being shut up in a room, that children play
with knucklebones, men with words, and where,
before they enter our lives, diseases lie

is a mystery? Silent veins of smoke
thread the air. Over the fields a clump
of houses appears, bristling with sound: notes
from a strident rooster, the mill's slow thump.
This is the village where children suckle on goats
and the poor hide their diseases with a cloak

of gentle words which relieve the pain and soften
their harshness. What would we do without names?
Worldly troubles are mostly grammatical
and we have taught our ladies' cheeks to flame
at the mere mention of what they are not at all
afraid to do. Sometimes in daylight. And often.

I could ride for hours: pacing does not tire
me as much as a set journey which forces
me straight ahead instead of the roads which chance
throws up. I think my ideas are like horses.
Sometimes they follow each other at a distance;
at others they glance sidelong at each other.

The path declines and we descend and muddy
hooves spatter our caparisons.
To what could I compare this river? A moulting
snake? What matter our comparisons
when this river, like a civil war, is revolting
against itself, eroding its banks? I study

the surface, shedding scales of light; beneath,
on the river-bed the wind's shadow furrows
its skin like a plough. I study everything:
what I must flee and that which I must follow,
although since my earliest days nothing
has occupied my mind more than death,

but I've never gnawed my nails over Aristotle.
Once, as I stood on the headland of my brother,
the Sieur d'Asac's lands in Médoc, I saw the waves
break over what was once his land. At another
time he had been rich: now, nothing save
fens and drains remain from his battle

with the sea. We continue over dunes
under puffed up clouds and pass a flotilla
of ducks quacking in tiny epicycles
on the current. I cannot stay still. A
mind does nothing but whirl around like little
silkworms which then get tangled in cocoons.

One and the same pace of my horse seems to me
now rough, now easy; the same road at one
time shorter, another time longer; one and the same
view now more, now less pleasing; the sun
now shines too hot, now too feeble a flame
to warm my tired bones. Now I am ready

to do anything, now to do nothing. I do
nothing but come and go and I'm unable
even to rid myself of vice, I just exchange
one for another. Only a fool is immovable
and certain. The sun has become a blazing orange
rising towards the meridian of depthless blue.

It's getting hot. I could stay all day
in the saddle, riding around and about without
flagging. Recently I've heard of a tribe
of cannibals in the new world. I do not doubt
there is more barbarity in eating a man alive
than dead; but who are we to talk, who flay

our enemies alive like dumb creatures
when they are men, like us? These cannibals
know valour; they would rather be killed and eaten
than ask not to be. To a man they are unable
to yield to fear: they are killed, not beaten.
But then again, they do not wear breeches.

A horn sounds. My neighbour hunts again.
Gentlemen are mounting their horses, eager
to course across the grounds and chase some hare,
petrified, and watch lean hounds crush meagre
bones and fur in their grim jaws. I share
the thrill of a hunt, but cannot stand the pain.

I steer my horse homewards — there is a shelf
in my circular library filled with books which say
the earth and planets revolve around the sun.
Perhaps that is the case. For every day
our fortunes change and turn around our sovereign
king. But I revolve within myself.

Velocity

A dying man's eyes alive
with the light of television.
Mushrooms, banished by light.
Shadows prop up capped roofs
or fall from gill-ribbed eaves.
A man dying, watching mushrooms,
Swiss browns like ragged penises,
the light of the television flaring
bluishly around his head: a halo
sprouting in the dark, invisible
to his gaze, caught up as it is
with mushrooms. A former boss appears
on the screen in an advertisement
for laxatives. He appears
not to have aged at all, the ex-boss, that is,
although television adds kilos,
subtracts years and scatters spores
of information in the dark.
He's still bald, the ex-boss,
although the man dying is not
that flush with hair either. From underneath
a dirty white toadstool scalp
the ex-boss tries to impose
his authority on people he can't see,
feeding them his image in the dark,
a straw mushroom with no hair
and a dirty beard, bear arms
a little like the prophet Elisha.
On the table is a letter
from another (only just!)
ex-boss, the form guide, the remote.

The man dying alone in the room
no longer feels entirely alone
even though nobody objects to
or remarks on his rapid transformation:
enoki toes, monkey-headed,
two Jews' ears, scaly teeth
and a flicking, russular tongue
and rolling around in his stalk-necked
head, two eyes like black diamonds
scan the screen which scans at twenty-four
frames per second, a single line
from top to bottom flinging
pixels to the four corners of the room.
He is all flesh, a springy cloud
flecked with points of green, red and blue
alone in a room with a television,
a table and on it a box bedded with straw
budding rapid globes, the whites
of upturned eyes. If he lives
long enough, he plans to change
his name: Morel, he thinks, or Mirabeau,
Teonanacatl or possibly Boletus.
He would walk to the registry office
in the shade of his parasol, wearing
a coolie hat, but given the speed
of his decline he must be content instead
to wait for the sudden flare of trumpets,
yellow chanterelles preferably,
which will announce his last vision:
a forest of upstarts burgeons out of nothing,
each trying to overshadow the other.

The Weed King

The Weed King dreams his Empire
and is taken there by minions
on a palanquin made of grass and nettles,
oxalis, clover and dandelion.
Through desert plains of prickly pear
on Spinifex wheels he rolls across the ground,
through paddocks gullied by cattle
and garlanded with Paterson's Curse
his grand procession, thistle-crowned,
takes its steady, remorseless course,

At the foot of impassable alps
he ascends in a puffball airship
piloted by propagules
and driven along the wind by seeds
of western salsify, box elder
and Empress tree. When he reaches the sea
he crosses on a raft of woven snakeweed;
at the verge of impenetrable forests,
on cat's claw and lantana he climbs the brakes.
Nothing is able to thwart his progress.

Everywhere the Weed King's minions
take him, he disperses lavishly:
multitudes are in his thrall
and sway in the breeze devotedly,
bend up to the sky in ecstatic admiration;
and wherever he is not, he has an interest,
his ways and laws prevail
and such is his magnificence
that even the mountains, trees and flowers bow down,
make way for his insatiable intelligence.

Tsunami

Beginning with a murmur
what will end under mountains of wet noise.
Like the way those thugs once held the tapered haft
of a baseball bat high and in reserve
over our heads
in a smash and grab:
a wave which didn't need to break
because it had already hollowed us out,
on Denison Street.

Or the poet who couldn't help himself
and satirised his nation's leader, shrugged his shoulders
but wouldn't, couldn't recant — not even when his teeth
were prised out, one by one, with a claw-hammer.
(How could it be otherwise? Poetry is rumour made permanent)
and his appeal to the least known of the muses, that of silence,
failed — and the endless murmuring
deep inside him
swept into a summit
and broke upon him from within,
dragging him back into oblivion.

TEARS

The categories are broken. In their stead
candles blaze and bleed, and a flurry of darkness
chases the light away across the walls.
Faces reappear in the carpet and melt
into animal shapes. Brisk insects maze
the air. The difference between purple and indigo
is about the same as that between occupation
and settlement. Impossible to tell in this light.

Not quite the same is ice afloat on water:
then it's ice or water, even though one
keeps melting into the other, like eyes
filling with water and slipping down a face
into a world which shrinks towards a word
and where, for a while, all boundaries are blurred.

Medusa

I drifted through the gallery of long arcades,
autistic with light. Headless models
and unframed masterpieces strained towards the air.
Most beautiful of all, the plaster walls
humming with a down of sun.
What once had colour was colourful still
but everything I'd loved had disappeared,
would disappear and vanish into stone.
Through the vague surrender
of seaweed, darkness stubborn as bone.
Patience is a dying art, something only stone understands.
Hidden from the cindering sun,
I was that stinging corona billowing wetly
and burning with remembered light.

Death by Water 1: Hippasos

'. . . he who first disclosed the knowledge of surds or irrationals and spread it abroad among the common herd perished by drowning'

Pappus, *Commentary on Euclid's* Elements X

Two
needs
drove him
to his end —
the perfect beauty
of a theorem and, hidden
within, the outrage of its inexpressible truth.

Disagreeing, the retribution they delivered was swift:
between his knowing and their need
for knowledge, he described
overboard
his death's
surd
arc.

Lagoon

This is where I come from if it's true
to say I come from somewhere not just
anywhere south of the Imagination,
where they came from, ended up,
warty hills of the Monaro
or an Irish quag.
It's Lagoon, with wind-tussocked, wrinkled
hills worn down to a murmur
that claims me.
Flat skied, convict-shaped
earth, the barren sweep
from Tannas Mount knuckled
with Bathurst quartz, small and obedient
noon shadows: this is where justice
jammed them, impatient and impenitent
forebears transported for a brace
of crimes: possession
of a stolen lamb,
highway robbery
and other, nameless filchings cancelled
by oblivion.
It's hard to tell exactly where
it was: the lagoon has forgotten
itself, drowned
under Chifley Dam's
green skin brailled by metallic rain,
or a mired bend in Campbell's River
where dragonflies whirr in a spectral frenzy
like solid drops of petrol darting in the sun.

I have inherited their future
born of silent massacres,
patient weathering
of the cold fastness of hills
and endurance of each summer's baked mirages.
They mastered the art of sticking
to the narrow furrows of their lives
whereas I have learnt
only the art of streets,
sailing between their guttered shores
on that new ocean, traffic.
Every trace of them has vanished.
There is a school there now,
where children, yet to learn
that dreams are what make death real,
play in the stark sun.
Horse studs
gather along the creek
and they stand there, fluid
flanks shiny in wintered light
chewing and staring down
impostors in their midst.
Time has stolen it,
evaporated family mysteries
like the slow death of a photograph
of the old farm,
like neap days
pinched of history.

Death By Water 2

It's little wonder I write about water.
Seven generations ago, having shot his load
of rum and sperm in Sydney Cove,
Stephen Tuckerman, Captain of the USS Carolina
disappeared off the coast of Chile with all his crew,
Lieutenant Neil McKellar of the NSW Corps,
despatches from Governor King and the sword
of Captain John Macarthur.
He left behind
an illegitimate son whose daughter,
Mary was widowed in 1856
when her husband, Thomas L'Estrange
drowned while attempting to swim on horseback
across the Cudgegong River then in flood.
The man who tried to rescue him
drowned as well. A raft was built
and eight men were awarded medals
in 1857 'in approval of exertions
made to recover the bodies of persons drowned.'
One of these eight was Harry Albury
whose grandson had Joe Wilson tell
of how he'd 'helped drag two bodies
out of the Cudgegong River in a flood,
and they weren't sleeping beauties.'

One hundred
and eight years later Thomas and Mary's grand-daughter
nursed me, her great-grandson, in her arms.
That's what happens with death by water:
fiction flows into fact, fact into fiction
and rising up in a flood of words
the past spreads out beyond the present,
carrying into life its drifting dead.

Dew

for Ben Fenton-Smith

None are more familiar with dew
than professional footballers. From early
grades they are used to running through
practice drills and hurling their burly
frames through rucks while the moist chaff
of wet grass under winter lights
softens their fall, accustoms the half-
back to the slippery ball and writes
green cuneiform on wet sandshoes.
And they fear it in the morning,
kicking off the dew in the 'twos'
because they ignored a coach's warning.
Half their lives are spent in clouds
of condensation or the cold heat
of a winter sun where even the crowds
seem like droplets on the concrete
rose of the stadium. In the final days
of their season, sweat-spangled on the eve
of their triumph, the ball on a string and their plays
honed, even the doubters believe.
And the last day is, once again,
already an aftermath: the ground's been shaved
and sucked dry by the noon sun
and the paddock has become a paved
and bristled hell for those who will
collide with it and pinion flesh on
earth, earth on flesh and spill
blood for the sake of a game. Possession
is the law; all are possessed.

And when the crowd melts into the dry
darkness, after that great red football's
booted between the uprights of the sky-
scrapers and gone, the sky bawls
cheerless little drops for the victors
and decks the oval with the losers' jewels.

The Swimmer: a cento

You waded in, embracing water,
taking its measure, mastering currents

disappearing into the black depths
    the broken columns, the outline of ancient streets
    and colonnades
mountain streams absorbed into the submerged city
where wavering masses bulge and gape
    the continuous dream of a world underwater
old palaces and towers
quivering within the wave's intenser day

then away he swam, the one who had survived
swam with his eyes open and it was green and dark
but out from the beach, from that margin of
smooth green water
there curves and glimmers outward to the unknown
the swift whirl of the new breaking wave
    green and glassy gulfs
and the sea flint-flake, black-backed in the regular blow

and the beautiful pea-green back-pasture
blows more strongly, the dark is turned to rags
having roughed up the waters,
wind explodes like loud curses from fist-ravaged lips
heaving with rage, swollen
sea-foam and the frothing of blood
and flood upon flood carries on, never ending

the scrumming surf broke over and blinded me
        swimming long in the abyss of thought
the stanching, quenching ocean of a motionable mind;
making for the open sea,
thrashing from side to side with strong, sure, professional strokes
as I swam with a thousand twists and turns,
like a stone across the surface with each stroke
striking the water and drawing it towards me

swimming towards the light

Waterlilies, Ueno Park

It's not the flat green plates puckered and racked
in tiers of frosted glaze or the people grazing

an empty ceramic picnic, or horn-mouthed carp
groping towards undrinkable air for bread

among the handles of green umbrellas inverted
in the sweaty park air that stays with you

but the wet coin of water rolling in the middle of a pad
or was it a lens still at the heart of a roving green eye?

The Baby Boomers

It is the present. The stars are almost as they were, unnameable
constellations imperfectly identified as bears,
a Pontiac convertible, a celtic cross, a seagull
or an albatross, by four friends gazing at attention
from the balcony of a holiday house on a nameless river
near the coast. It's where they've come to stay after the wedding
of some other friends, 'joining in early autumn light'
despite the summer heat. Temporary, fragile derricks
pump red oil from their uncovered limbs and then take off,
syrinxing around their ears. The Hunter Valley cabernet
is almost gone; whiffling up from the river, the therapeutic
sound of tiny waves shiatsuing the shore. Property
is their new religion, they are its breathless acolytes;
the cogwheels of their conversation, negatively geared
are running back towards the day's quiet revolution, sleep.

Morning ploughs the living room through blinds.
They surface like pink bathyspheres and float around the house.
The birds zoom in and out of trees, cicadas fume noise.
Midriffs, thighs, creased earlobes, whiskered jowls: municipally pink.
Grey-timbered trees erupt in vivid, yellow-throated song.
Julie flexes, stretches studiously, sexually important.
Sounds without name move among the forest-floor leaves.
Tinkle of spoons on plates, the slamming fridge, the toaster ballista.
An osprey gathering up the day, lifting it higher, motionless.
After showers patinas of sweat keep on returning.

On stilts: the timber holiday house sounding
the steep escarpment down to the morning river bank;
flavour walking through their midday meal,
a Julie special, she cannot judge the quantities;
Tony almost walks on water, sagging in the rivermud
as he attempts a circus crossing, a rehearsal
to impress the kids later on; their conversation —
they haven't been together, in a group,
without children for quite some time.
So alcohol's their lantern, over Pictionary®;
inspiration bulbs and dims, invigorates the old
alliances, the new conceits, the rediscovered myths.

Every now and then a thought occurs to them:
the sky is in pieces (it must be something
a witchdoctor said) with nothing in between.
How do they know this? Because they remember
the fitting apart, the falling together
decades ago, which is another country.

Barry lifts the lid on past invention,
the masses' stoichiometry, the city's ravelled streets.
It sort of all coheres, as cold air gathers
underneath the fridge, because it leaks
and cobwebs billow slyly at its back.
There's a recipe for depression,
tailored just for him. How did they know?
His heart is in the right place, so they tell him,
it's his eyes . . . cross-eyed and clueless,
'the people' cheer him on! In an avocado suit
he braves the waves, thinking 'what if
money were see-through? The emperor's new notes?'
A thousand gulls are recrudescing on the beach.
Where will it end, the waves' instinctive violence,
the sweep of galactic arms into nothingness?

Debbie lobsters lazily inside all afternoon:
is it super that she's worried about or the complement
of what they do not have? Barry promised everything
and almost got there. Almost: that leaves out gravity,
against which she's been waging war for years. Horizontally,
or lifted by a wave, she's shackled by it and, what's worse,
she knows she's in the wrong, and it is right. That's why she smokes,
she privately admits, that and monumental boredom.

Barry cannot read. He used to, but no longer. His brain
refuses, point-blank, like a mule. He'll put it out to graze
on newsprint, novels, channel-surfing, traffic signs and menus
but it demurs, skips to the end, seeks out the passing cleavage.
He doesn't even read his own reports, they're fiction anyway,
and have a growing readership: he hates the demographic.
From time to time he'll hover over the paper, skimming the stars.

Tony *is* technology, he sometimes thinks aloud,
in the third person. That's why Julie's carnal empire
interests him, he thinks of it as one long line of code:
SetConnect = Julie.CreateObject Connect.Open
    'IntimateConversation'
Intimate.Conversation.SetName = 'Luscious Pie'
Query = "SELECT * FROM Luscious Pie"
Query = Query & "WHERE Mood = 'concupiscent' AND Light
    = 'Candle'
Option Explicit On
Option Strict On
INSERT into 'Luscious Pie' VALUES 'yes' 'more' 'please' 'again'
Response.Write "aaah"

She can't understand how they have suddenly grown old.
The Julie thing was its peak when kumera was king,
pesto its prince and sun-dried tomatoes were almost de rigeur,
the currency of chic. Pediments were pastel,
'postmodern' was a seasoning she used to spice her works:
buildings the shade of eyeliner and blush; the neo-, pseudo-
classical porticoes, non-primary colours. And plinths.

Now it's all passé; the flavourings have changed, the money
is the same and she looks young, despite the fact she isn't.
Design is a drug, it cures the future of banality:
that's what she does; her ageing edifices keep her young,
and hungering after clean lines, she architects a world
where holidays are R&D, or so says her accountant.

Debbie lights another gold-tipped cigarette and lies
back on the foam mattress. It's so hot, Barry dissolves
ice cubes in his beer. The sky is bubbling like a spoon
and there's a war in the Gulf. Again. This time they're not sure
whose side they're on or even if there are sides. Tony says
his Volvo has a cold. Imagine that! Girl in Coma
Writes Novel, the radio seems to say, or maybe it's
a line from a Latin American poet without subtitles,
or something like that. Once they used to walk about naked
but an avalanche of flesh means that history now repeats
itself, like that blimp recurring through the palms, saying,
Mozart. Is that a liqueur, Julie wonders, or just a tropical
whatever, himself or cosmic radiation, she's so out of touch.
Even here they are in the suburbs. Who cares about the wedding
cake or the religion hidden between the jokes? Like furry scabs,
flies encrust the drink-rings on the table and a periscope
impales the air. Is it Nemo on the verge of surfacing
or a swizzle-stick out of all perspective? Like tattered underwear,
too many questions hang limply in the air. Cornelius Toad
to Secret Squirrel, are you reading me, over? But Tony's leaning
sideways as he slaloms around a bend and doesn't hear
(Dirtbox Megadeath III, the Final Reckoning) and Barry's off

on a tangent anyway, his chest hurts from reading far too much
about cigarettes or the sublime 'again' in Heidelberg
School light, or maybe it's just Debbie giving him a hard time
about his deafness. When did everyone learn to speak Russian?
Poems lie around the room, stiff as ruined joints.
I was beautiful once, says Julie, and quite probably sane.

The river keeps rebooting. An empty crate rebels against
the tide. A yellow scum plaques the river's banks and glides,
like a future thick with disappointment, downstream. The present
has been smoking for some time without any sign
of dissolving into flame. Photographs without colour
pulse on unctuous water. The question is not, 'is it
art?' but how much it is worth, so Barry reckons. An opal
irritated out of clouds, the moon drops into their drinks
and Julie, agape at the stars, starts to get quite sentimental
when she thinks how violently they burn, how long
they've blazed before they all were born and how, despite surviving
them for several billion years, even the stars will die.
Debbie, stalled above a chessboard in her fat bikini,
sarong and sandals, stoops to conquer Barry's white — it's mate.
He's saddened there's no antidote for perfect beauty.
While they go on waiting, Tony's aliens respawn.
Like another 'situation' years ago, they're younger than they think.
He coughs and a cloud begins to weep on Julie, on the deck
a shiny rash appears, becomes a beating film advancing
towards the double doors, and still the children haven't called.

Daylight Saving

Low in the clear
sky the sliver, the spotty scimitar
of the moon: necrotizing clouds gather
and drift, zooming swiftly
across it, lit with the noon
of another timezone,
where outsourced call centres hum
in dusty cities, calling
telephones in empty homes,
homes emptied of appetite,
emptied of brawling
desires — they're all in the park, dumb
with serious worship
of the last free bits of light.

The Well

for Bill Dunbar

Not choked yet, the well persists
in a flurry of unbecoming
leaves and sinews of a baroque
vine whose pendant harmonica-
ribbed pods rattle and scrape
the shelved neck of river
rocks like lobes hanging heavy
with jewellery; surmounting
the mouth a hipped party-hat
roof dangles a streamer
bucketed metres down with water.
May flies obituarise
themselves in busy lines and summer
foretells its own demise
in dense explosions of chlorophyll.
Floored by the heat neither
frogs nor pleasure prosper
but, busy trapping light,
spiders transform leaves
from outside to interior
with a predatory intricate curling.
Aiming for the stagnant mirror
of the garden pond the sun
misses and instead strikes
the horizon. Mosquitos mass on the border
of night and day and launch
their sorties through the heavy

lingerie of elephant's
ear, the phosphorescent wake
of snails and their faint
fury. Over it all the moon
presides in its high black bench,
blind and stern and fattening
on what it keeps
for itself, its cold and necessary
justice. Otherwise
nights would bleed into sparse dawns
and the sun would rise
like a guillotine, only to fall
at noon down the deep
pit of the well. Strange, isn't it,
how the well is always
full and how the spray of cicada-
song leaves you perfectly
dry; stranger, though, is how
the bucket, like the pre-
dawn sun, seems to come up
before it has risen, ablaze
with subterranean glistening,
clearing the snarled throat
of the well with a slight wobble,
a slight splash of the new.

Bodies of Water

There are not enough words to utter all your fleeting names, O water
Wisława Szymborska, 'Water'

I've surfed your waves, body-
surfed I mean, surging
through quarrelling foam
onto sand, a polished
twist of driftwood. I've sniffed
your fine capillaries
from where the sky breathes mist
onto mountains, to where
the mountains shrug off creeks,
the closed groin
of valleys veined with them
to backward flowing ripples
on brackish tidal reaches.

I've seen the ocean
and its indifference throwing up
heights and filling in
its restless excavations —
it's a light sleeper.

I've watched your grey clouds
sweat rain, leaf-gilding rain
tossed free with a flick
of the wind, and gyres
of steam rising from summer roads.

And even when I'm taking off,
climbing through your velvet clouds,
slumped in aviophobia,
words, inadequate skyhooks,
go on tethering: torn bread
clouds on a burnished platter,
palm-sweat, drowning eyes,
slow-mo waves below, curling
white window-corner mist,
wing-tips scoring vapour
through the dry heavens,
the horizon's wet blade.

I've seen how, like a dream
that keeps returning
we move from state to state,
water flowing through us,
we through water,
a consciousness, a breath.

Seaweed

Sometimes out of the wet hillocks
a ragged company heaves and settles
in a prickly flush and weave
of beads and beards and weird limbs.

Riddled by fish, the seaweed moves
within itself, a loitering detail
of shredded uniforms and snorkel-stems
swishing towards, away from the beach.

It's only when the sea tips over
in falling walls of white and green
that dark gorillas raise up their arms,
standing up in surrender, or is it praise?

Odyssey

Ripples knitted by day undone
by darkness: for ten years
Odysseus keeled that soft body,
not knowing that his end was one
with his means. In Ithaca, finding many

instead of the one, he took his revenge,
knowing how she awaited him still,
wind-charmed and unfathomable:
the ever-many, the sun-deceiving,
faithful, all-embracing sea.

Freeman's Reach, Hawkesbury River

for J.W.

Out of the silence, a team of ducks
lands on the river with a whoosh
of compression braking, drowning
out the sound of cattle chewing
on the other bank. From around
the bend a speedboat lamely chugs
upstream, then turns away, its wake
a tightening knot on the river's stillness.

Poplars quiver like yellow whips.
Bee-racked, rising out of thick grass,
castor-oil plants brandish their pods,
tiny red grenades armed with green pins.
Behind us, a hill mined by rabbits bares
its guts behind a retaining wall
of chicken wire.
                    Half a rampart,
the ironbark jetty warps over water
and, standing at its end, a poet
completely surrounded.

Evaporation

Do not look at a picture for too long, do not read a book too intently, do not listen to a piece of music with the greatest intensity. You will ruin everything for yourself, and thus the most beautiful and the most useful things in the world. Thomas Bernhard

The hospital where you were born,
its cream-coloured rooms, the slanting light;

blinding hillocks of salt,
years spent over an empty page;

the vast flood plain, the scored bed
and an obedient line of cows

trudging through a blizzard of light
to the remnants of the river;

the size of a body, a bone dry trench;
pillars supporting an empty sky;

after the ink has dried, words,
this book and those you love, you.

Ice

Morning fangs eaves and rinks roads
glittering black. Clouds grind across
distant mountains, weighed down by loads
of white slurry. The sun sets its course

through the frozen ecliptic — and walking out
in the cracking cold, crunching thwart
stalks and steering between mangy pelts
of snow, I am alone in the crackling silence,

the auditor of silent cries. Hanging upside-
down from trees, tapers drip cold
light onto a mass of frozen white
abstraction. And in it I am desolate and old

and a little bit grumpy with feet aching in slush.
The wet blaze of the sun skating across
blinding archipelagos of white flesh
melting, evaporating . . . it taunts me, this effortless

convulsion of the day's eye. These are the states
through which we pass: of breath become
solid, of body melting away, sublimate.
L'état c'est moi: the frozen core of the flame.

Carphology

n. Delirious fumbling with bedclothes

Afloat on the crushed ocean of our sleep
we could be those shipwrecked souls,
les naufrages, marooned by the imperfection
of dreams and eyeing each other
hungrily. Or jaunty in command,
steering by the sphered
armillary of our joining,
we sail across rippled sheets for love's far horizon.
This is our grand sleep. It fills up
our sails, knows no anchors
(they are all old, anyway),
takes weeks, months, digs in
to the day and carries us,
fumbling mutineers, delirious with the dark
sun of dreams, to a new Pitcairn.
We will never find sleep's
lost Europe in these ample folds
nor ever require it, nor ever cross
those currents set between us. They carry
us on in night's inverted ocean
past the bubbled constellations
of fish-eyed stars and the shooting trails
of garfish, a winnowed blink of bait
and the mullet's mad plop. We run on alone,
three sheets to the wind on passion,
one for our mingled breathing,
two for our solitude,
three for the surface of dreams
shattered each morning
adrift on tangled sheets.

The Eye

sits on an idea
like a city on its contours,
sharpening lights and slanting shadows.
Inside it lurk dark pockets:
its blind spot clouds the sky.

This city plays the fool; a nasty fool
with loaded fists and sullen flesh
who's hatched an ugly starburst on my face.

The inanely beautiful world goes on:
trees bend and flutter, plums draw the future
into swelling wholes,
taxis graze the streets.
My eye, a hungry nomad,
ranges through the shadow music of the city,
mind-shaded and flat,
cloud-brewed and vengeful,

searching lachrymal corners,
leaving an eye-shaped hole
wherever it lights, hunting
a vision into its socket.

The Osage Orange

for Simon West

Winter is blooming
                    damp, steak-coloured
toadstools and leaves,
                    papery verso,
purplish fingerprints recto thick on a vine —
a fit gift for a homecoming or calming a house.
                                        Thick humus
ebbs from stone garden walls
and human ornamentals pop up all over the grounds
of Heide's modernism. There's a desert in its sky,
orange leaching westward;
                    unmoored and floundering
we're like snuff poets
                    in search of a subject,
wandering about and as uneasy
                              as if we had found one.

In the gallery inside
               monumental art of modern terror
at a safe remove
          still cows a little,
                              depresses a little more
and leaves us bleakened: a version of art which doesn't redeem
but warns or distils: the statue of a judge
looming high over buildings,

only just smaller than the sky,
the broken man on the pier
and the man on the broken pier
or the broken man, running along a disintegrating pier,
wide-eyed and shrieking
and in the distance, the size of a mountain,a ship
drifts, menacing
like diplomacy
ancient or modern.

Marmoreal fragments:
the trunk of a lion
caged in glass
is art;
the uncaged lion in the hotel foyer
framed by plate-glass windows is also art;
a sea of wires and girders,
shelled buildings,
Stalingrad chic,
remind us: unfinished wonders are the best art of all.

The unenjoyable game
of the world that wakes at night
and harrows the field of dreams
with foreboding lines
and ready-made scars
fleshes its anxiety with a canniness that bleeds

into the day and almost terrifies,
dissipates
like the experience of recognising your own viscera
burst and shrink in ultrasound
like a wet, clever war.

Outside the wind vowels and thistles
and we walk in the garden,
your skull flowering
black silver ringlets
and you pick up one rotting Osage orange
and then another, pure green and monkey-brained
and turn it over in your hand
as St Jerome might have rolled his skull
around in his hands,
as if its green wrinkles
incarnate a truth
memento mori
memento ludi
unlike the cunning smooth of bone,
a dome convolved with words —
it is a shy brain which fears its subtle folds and what it arranges,
as if it would unbecome itself
be somehow inside-outed,
that something would erupt from it
if it was slammed into the earth
again
and again.

We left them there,
                    half-shattered and oozing,
damaged wholes
               and we drove back to the city
along the scoured gouge of freeway.
Sparsely skewered streetlights flickered on,
and beyond the pecuniary rods and spires,
the west lit up
             with a seeping flame,
                                        a faint livid bursting
tipped with orange and gold, a cloud-streaked wort
blossoming there, uncurled and lingering, almost whole.

Coledale

How did the world get so small?
How could it be contained within one book?
Because we have authored it ourselves,
written in kisses,
caresses plunging us deeper into that careful story
of passion,
            like the waves at Coledale
slowly emerging from the dreaming sea,
the curves of young skin stretching out of sleep
or darkness rising out of the earth,
rising up from the sea
in outcrops of moon-foam
and, leaping up over cold rocks,
star-fallen swell
                        reaching up in plumes of desire.

Port Hacking, South-West Arm

Commanding knowledge greater than the pin-pricks
of its eyes allow, neck erect, Egyptian-like
and ruddering strongly in a straight line,
undercutting the ever-changing dimpled peaks,
the salt-oil brimmings and shallowings,
the slender snake crosses the south-west arm
of the port, already in full possession of the other side.

Splash

Bored in the office again
tracing an old coffee stain:

this is how my mind is,
a teeming sphere smashed
on the page, again and again.

Postcards from a Drought

1

A pair of exercise bikes
parked on a concrete slab
in the front yard of the house
in the middle of the harrowed plain.

2

Bore water lashing
the grass and the daisies,
a green iris
in a bloodshot eye.

3

Umbrella grass lost
in the corners of sheds,
piled high to the ceilings:
an ossuary of fine, spoked bones.

4

A busy highway
beginning somewhere out back
ends at the biscuit jar,
jammed with ants.

5

A bust of Voltaire
smiles too much
in a dusty sunroom
stacked with leather suitcases.

6

Wood pigeons and wasps
drink from the covered bathtub.
Lowing warily, starved of grass,
cattle graze the lawn.

7

Bowsers for water, petrol
and oats. From the road,
fine dust storms leap
over them and vanish.

8

Eight linked maidens
dance around the outside
of a stained cement urn. Frogs
inside it croak like prophets.

9

Making love in the afternoon,
trying for a child; almost at random
white butterflies flower
over coarse lawn.

10

Venus wakes us up at 3 a.m.
intrudes among the trees
and then ascends,
dwindling.

11

On the fourth day of Christmas
crows rise
from pepper trees
and stain the grid, the dust.

12

A dead tree quivering:
a bird springs into
a bush. And then resumes
its funerary.

13

Wires have disappeared
from the telegraph poles.
Everything goes underground
in this heat.

14

Sundial in shadow,
spare clouds drift.
Buried at its base,
grandparents' ashes.

15

An ancient woman forgets
the name of her daughter-in-law.
Wet ice slips
in an empty wine glass.

16

In the distance cars hover
on liquid haze
and sink
into the dry road.

Rain

is how the earth pleads
with the sky. It offers up
its thirst and the sky responds,
showers its bounty
in bunched drops
that sluice and scatter.
On a hot day
steam springs
in small coils of gratitude.
Dew
is how the sky teases
the earth, a pretend rain
spun out of air
which says no
downfall is final,
nor is it ever enough.
And when it rains
the earth still aches:
it is never enough,
still it is never enough.

Poetry in print from John Leonard Press

2006	
A bud	*Claire Gaskin*
Cube Root of Book	*Paul Magee*
Ocean Island	*Julian Croft*
The Passion Paintings: Poems 1983-2006	*Aileen Kelly*
2007	
Vertigo | a cantata |	*Jordie Albiston*
The Incoming Tide	*Petra White*
Letters to the Tremulous Hand	*Elizabeth Campbell*
Man Wolf Man	*L K Holt*
2008	
Poems 1980-2008	*Jan Owen*
White Knight with Bee Box: New and Selected Poems	*Peter Steele*
Growing Up with Mr Menzies	*John Jenkins*
Therapy Like Fish: New and Selected Poems	*Marcella Polain*
2009	
Collected Poems	*Vincent Buckley* ed. *Chris Wallace-Crabbe*
The sonnet according to 'm'	*Jordie Albiston*
White camel	*Morgan Yasbincek*
Pilbara	*Mark O'Connor*
Marriage for Beginners	*Catherine Bateson*
2010	
The Simplified World	*Petra White*
Patience, Mutiny	*L K Holt*
Phantom Limb	*David Musgrave*

JOHN LEONARD PRESS